C000040423

From Here to Timbuktu

From Here to Timbuktu

Pauline Plummer

Published 2012 by
Smokestack Books
PO Box 408, Middlesbrough TS5 6WA
e-mail: info@smokestack-books.co.uk
www.smokestack-books.co.uk

From Here to Timbuktu
Pauline Plummer
Copyright 2012, by Pauline Plummer, all rights reserved
Author photograph: Trevor Cook

Printed by
EPW Print & Design Ltd

ISBN 978-0-9568144-4-9

Smokestack Books is
represented by Inpress Ltd
www.inpressbooks.co.uk

for Boubacar Traoré, Malian blues guitarist
from a fan

thanks to Dot Lee and Christine Harrison
who encouraged me to finish when I felt like giving up

'Indeed there's little pleasure for your bones
Riding along and all as dumb as stones.'

Prologue to *The Canterbury Tales*, translated by Neville Coghill

Part I

When Europe groans with the sullen weight
Of winter clouds and frozen naked trees
And noonday sky is washed in lemon light,
We long to follow where the southern breeze
Lifts the swallows over lakes and seas
To where the sky spreads cobalt blue
Like a wedding sheet round Timbuktu.

The endless pressures of our working lives
Stifle us. We dream and long to free
Ourselves of children, husbands, wives
So for a hefty sum the company
Will sort adventure holidays in Mali
With tents and porters, cooks and guides
Across savannah in a four-wheel drive.

We're tourists from a range of English
Speaking countries. We journey far
Beyond the ordinary because we're rich
Enough to travel through the Sahara
And sneer at holidays that we'd think kitsch
And commonplace. No, that just won't do;
We'll grin and bear the road to Timbuktu.

We seem somewhat exhausted and time-poor.
We obey the gods of work and earning cash
But now we want to go where life is raw
And take a little risk, be slightly rash,
Drink palm wine and maybe smoke some hash.
We'll see how people live at slower speeds
And question our exaggerated needs.

The Mali women sway in dazzling colour
Gowns as if they owned the dusty ground
They walk on. Songhai, Peul and Fula,
Bambara and Dogon – we'll hear the sound
Of many ancient languages but dollars,
Euros, pounds and francs will speak for us
As we're driven in our air-conditioned bus.

Annoyingly our airplane is delayed;
We get at first to know each other's names
And countries and those who'd irritate
And those who'd play the shaky friendship game.
We slowly learn some simple facts, no shame
Or tragedies or traumas just the boring stuff
Careers and cities lived in, that's enough.

At last we take the Air France flight to Bamako.
Our 4x4 takes us to Mandé hotel
And we dine on French cuisine not local *toh*
And wash it down with Chardonnay, chilled well.
We're silent – spare with things to share and tell
But there's swimming in the lamp-lit pool
Where precious water's filtered fresh and cool.

Finally we meet our guides so lean and fit;
They're toned and tanned from all the treks.
Inez, the skinny Spanish woman hits
It off with all the men whose unruly sex
Is stirred by her in shorts and stretchy vest.
Dark-eyed, long-haired she's pretty and petite.
She has a smile of white and sharpened teeth.

Ben the other guide is English and polite.
He'll jolly us along to hide the fact
He hasn't done his homework and he's quite
At sea on information. His friendly act
Will charm us like his gentle sense of tact.
'Don't whine and whinge,' he'll say 'about your lot.
You knew it would be suffocating hot.'

So who is on this trip? From the US
Rick's a lawyer from the sunshine state
Who wears a cheap and uncool Walmart vest
And Cubans are the people whom he hates.
He takes on only cases that will make
Him rich and is irritated that his taxes go
To shiftless folk who live on welfare dough.

He's fifty but he doesn't have a wife
Just dates a string of pretty girl-friends
But dumps them when he's bored – a fun-filled life
Where thrilling pleasure doesn't have an end.
Commitment free. Like an oyster you depend
Upon yourself – buy health, install a gym
To build up pecs plus pool for daily swims.

Mike's a Londoner who deals in land
And property. He's in the know and makes
A profit by a legal sleight of hand.
He buys from those who've lost then takes
His time to see how much the market makes.
He came from East End poverty in Bow
But lives in luxury in Pimlico.

He's bought the very best in cameras
To document in style this scenic trip:
Wide screen to capture beast or human drama,
Zooms to snap tattoos on cheeks and lips.
His travel gear is crease-resistant hip.
Don't bother him with boring observations
Unless you have some left-field information.

Jasmine is the arts administrator
Successful through her taste and charm and guile.
Her Shoreditch flat has very little furniture;
The walls are painted white or grey. 'That's style,'
She says, eyeing people's painfully vile
Clothes. She knows who's cool, who's in, who's out,
Who's scene and puts herself to schmooze about.

She contemplates the crowded mini bus
And the need to share in two-bed tents.
'I find this rather dreadful. I really must
Refuse the plan. I need one to myself.
What if a fellow tourist farts or sweats?
Or what if someone's tedious or crude?
I haven't time for ignoramus dudes.'

'You'll have to take it as it comes,' says Ruth.
Her father was from Ghana: she's mixed race.
Her adoptive mother's from up North
And white. And though she doesn't tell the truth
She hardly knew her dad and not her roots
In Africa. She wishes she was really dark
And works on this with sun beds' UV arc.

She works in inner city Liverpool
With kids whose lives have drifted, mainly black.
She tries to get them back to normal school
Away from smoking ganja, skunk and crack
And gangs and violent failure, all that crap.
Her laughter and her swinging braided hair
Present a gaiety that isn't there.

Jay leans against the tourist travel bus
We'll travel in along the roads of Mali.
His face is weather-beaten; he'll cuss
A lot you'll see but he'll have had a belly
Full of moaning, spoilt tourists who fully
Understood there'd be no luxury hotels
Along the ancient routes of the Sahel.

From Ireland there's the zealous teacher Finn
Who's never had much zeal for making cash.
Though always laughing he is hurt within.
His gaze is dreamy. 'I need to turn my back
From children on the wrong side of the tracks.
Perhaps I'm in a rut, the endless job, the life.
I'm keen to wander now I've lost my wife.'

His clothes are crinkled, worn and loose;
His hair flops on his broad and freckled face.
He wears his ancient Gore-Tex walking boots
And drinks Malian beer by the case.
With i-pod on he thinks about his fate,
A happiness he'd had, a much loved wife,
Lost when cancer dragged her from this life

Renee adds she also won't be sharing tents
Any time soon and pulls her Zara t shirt
Over Dior jeans. She skilfully pretends
She's younger than her sixty three, still flirts
With her face-lifted smile – swivels her pert
Silhouette toned through workouts in the gym.
New York requires all women to be slim.

She's stringy rather, obsessed with what
She eats. Fish she's heard will give
Longevity and brain cells. Yoghurt
Skimmed of fat, milk thistle keeps her liver
Clean – her eyes are clear – not a sliver
Of cake will ever pass her plumped-up lips.
She swings on her best-buy, plastic hips.

She teaches dance, still flexes like a snake
And has a reptilian disposition.
She wants to know who's scene, who's on the make
Makes sure she knows the competition.
Age won't affect her skills as a tactician.
She's given parties for Big Apple's best.
Bob Dylan dropped by once as vaunted guest.

She married up – Manhattan's coolest pair
In town. He was something big in bonds
Venturing on brassy cash that wasn't there,
Rolled toxic assets, sucking oxygen
From normal fiscal life – the Napoleon
Of money speculation: obscene
To think that we must live within our means.

The flat in Central Park; the house in Maine,
The yacht, suits made for an oligarch,
The holidays in Fiji – the private plane,
Senators he'd bought and drove and parked,
Bank accounts offshore, investments in Bangkok.
Who cares we leave a legacy of debt?
I'm worth it. It's business. Abort regret.

'Wealthy men glow for predatory women,'
Says Renee. 'They smell cash and what it brings.
I bored him by being tragedienne
Over his affairs – his gifts of bling
To actresses and singers and other minx.
I unpicked his phone and found there texts
From yet another glamorous mistress.

'Well alimony for a wronged wife's fair.
I found a clever lawyer and with skill he plucked
The turkey clean. I took my legal share.
He was eviscerated but not fucked.
More money dealing to flavour what he'd cooked.
I moved to Boho, edgy, cool New York
And returned to dancing. Where were you, dork?'

'Well sweethearts like you are just the reason I stay
Single,' Rick shakes his head. 'I'm new money.
It's been grafted for in tough times night and day.
I'm not giving it away! Plenty lovely honeys
Who like to pass the time with me. I'm funny
And smart and useful if their papers aren't
What could be called legit. I've got a heart!'

'Well,' says Renee, smoothing on some hand cream
To ease the wrinkles puckered on the back.
'You'd be better off in Mali as its laws seem
To favour men with rights to own a stack
Of wives they have the right to sex and thwack.'
'It's not that stark,' Inez injects knowing that
The guides are listening to this vicious chat.

Lee's factory job is based in making snacks,
In Peterlee, where jobs are hard to find at all.
His mates take holidays in Spain. *He's cracked*
They say, *the places that he travels, Nepal*
Peru and now Mali. What an effing oddball.
Lee lives still in his ageing parents' house.
He's never found the guts for marriage vows.

He'll take photos of the lady from the arts
Or have one taken by another woman's side
And claim she was his holiday romance.
By, she looks posh, was she any good a ride?
Is she likely to become your blushing bride?
His clothes are wrong for never-ending heat:
Polyester trousers, nylon shirts but neat.

'I wonder why you're going on this trip,'
Says Finn to Lee. 'It seems a magic place
This Timbuktu. When I was just a kid
And being bad my mam would pack my case
To send me there like going into outer space.
I've saved up for a long time from my pay
From making crisps through shifts both night and day.

And the women are right beautiful,' he says.
'Sure that's a fact,' says Finn. 'Their backs must be
Erotic zones. They wear their dresses backless.'
'I'm interested in what tattoos they have,' says Lee
'I have a lot myself.' He rolls up his sleeves.
Two white arms with mythic animals and birds.
Hambo the driver's shocked and lost for words.

Martin doesn't wear his collar here.
His mufti hides his calling as a vicar.
Although he loves the swish of priestly gear
Non-religious people like him quicker
Without that. You'll see his nervous flicker
About something else he'd rather hide
That will be spotted on the lengthy ride.

Ursula's the poet on this curious adventure.
She's left behind her husband number three
And looks for new material, a venture
Into narrative, something she aspires to be
Financially successful and bring glory.
Her current spouse has empty pockets too.
She must profit from her trip to Timbuktu.

Part II

'Hey up,' says Ben our tall and jolly guide.
'I hope you're going to prove good company
And have some jokes to tell along the ride.
The roads are potholed and the stops are many
Let's try to keep our stories short or funny.
Here's my guitar to make a song or two
For the journey on the route to Timbuktu.'

'Oh no,' says Jasmine, 'what's the point of songs
By amateurs? So sixties, don't you think?
Those hairies thinking they would right the wrongs
By wearing tat and oils that made them stink
And hair that made them like the missing link.
The music here is good, on Radio Three
They play kora from the maestro Doubati.'

'It's ten days till we get to Mopti docks
And then the five we sail in the pirogue
Along the river Niger, till we reach our stop
In Timbuktu. Thus the end of our prologue.
Time to tell your stories in RP or brogue,
Your triumphs, joys and life's reverses,
You loves and sinfulness in crafted verses.'

Fateha speaks out, 'You've left me off
Your list. I mostly travel by myself
From Galapagos to frozen Rostov.
I'm a GP in the UK National Health.
My parents worry that I'm on the shelf.
They came from Bangladesh for well paid work
To give us opportunities and perks.'

Fateha is highly skilled and earns a lot
So no surprise she wants to see the world
And shop for stunning artefacts. She's not
Afraid of haggling for a bargain nor scared
Of crossing cultural borders. She'll wear
A jihab in a mosque but sip a tonic
In a pub with friends who like to drink.

'We're here to tell our jealous friends we've been
To Timbuktu,' say Chris and Tony, partners
Since they met at uni, over fifteen
Years ago. They work inventing charters
For Councils. She's a manager, a tartar
To her underlings. He's milder mannered
Introverted with a bashful stammer.

She's squat and stout and wears tight shorts
With boots. Malians in their flowing robes
Do not approve of this and think she ought
To cover up – those shameless *toubabus.*
She always grabs the best seat in the bus
And snatches food before the rest is served.
Has her mild partner got what he deserved?

Tony carries binos on his skinny arm
In case he sees an egret or a hawk.
It's the only thing that rumples up his calm
Or lights his pale blue eyes, or leads to talk.
A bulbul or a vulture make him gawp.
The kaleidoscope of myriads of birds
Makes his shrivelled heart swell up in words.

Ruth asks if people want to walk with her
To buy cloth in the market, then she'll find
A tailor making bubus, tops and skirts
To wear in the fierce heat. Ben's of a mind
To go, he swears local clothes, loose and lined
Are best – just wear what Malians do –
Bubus are cooler, bright and cheerful too.

'How ridiculous.' Chris sips the icy beer
She grabbed from off the tray and wouldn't pass.
'I've bought my Lands End shorts and travelling gear.
What! Sailing like a gaudy, loud *pinasse*?'
'The men in gowns and turbans do have class,'
Says Jasmine, 'but you won't see me in sarongs.
White sham – tasteless as a Charver thong.'

Ben and Ruth choose their patterned textiles
From the bolts of wax print and tie dye.
The merchant makes them tea while they choose styles
And they get measured watched by passers-by.
The tailor bends his skull-capped head and plies
The pedals on the Chinese made machine.
The needle pings; the whirring metal gleams.

The market smells of herbs, dried fish and tea.
They walk through stacks of rice, onions, sorghum
And see the gris gris stall – snake skins, monkey
Paws and claws of wild cat. Ruth feels welcome
Here, in touch with what she'd like to think her home
But isn't – the Africa she could've had
Went with the disappearance of her dad.

Ben returns in red and purple shirt
And cut-offs. 'At last I'm feeling cool and fresh
I hope I haven't missed the wisdom of your words,'
He says, ordering a beer and sliding on the bench.
'Holy mackerel you look colourful – a jolly mensch,'
Says Rick. 'Will you wear them when you're back
In Berkshire chasing foxes on horseback?'

And so we have forgotten Dieter Fromm
Who's older than the other tourists here.
He's travelled from the German town of Bonn
To shop for Dogon masks, carved wood and silver
Jewellery and his haggling takes forever.
To tell the truth he's crafty what he offers
Knowing he can make some tasty profits.

Dieter sighs and swigs his mineral water.
'I'll tell you if you need a story. It's true,
A story set in time of bloody slaughter.
When my mother died some years ago
I was bereft. I'd always loved her so.
But on her deathbed she whispered she had lied.
I wasn't after all her true-born child.

'My father had run factories in the war
Where Polish women had been sent to slave.
Among the girls was one he lusted after
Most. Was it rape or did she have to save
Her life through sex with a man she didn't love?
The Germans lost and did she then decide
To flee back home without her bastard child?

'I don't know what my father told his wife
Or if he begged forgiveness for unfaithful-
Ness? Maybe, but there was now a life
To care for. It might be she was grateful
For her married life had not been fertile.
She brought me up as if she was my mother,
A single child, no sister nor a brother.

'I didn't look like either mum or dad
And later when an adult thought I might
Have genes from unknown Russian lads
Who'd raped my mother. But my father died
Without a word to say how he had lied.
As Mutti aged and heard the scythe of death
She whispered things to me with her last breath.

'She told me which town my Polish mother came
From and her surname. I began to search
For many years. Of course I fought with blame
And anger at the story – but the itch
Would not be scratched until I ditched
My false identity and met up with my real
Family – then only would my grief be healed.

'Because my mother's marriage had gone sour
She'd reverted to her maiden name so
With help I found her back in Warsaw
With two sisters who I didn't know.
The language was so hard I learned it slow
But gradually I tried to make my life a part
Of theirs and wrap myself into their hearts.

'The life in Poland then was really hard
Whereas we Germans in the freer west
in our *gemutlich* homes, designer cars
Holidays abroad, felt coats, the very best
Of hifis and TVs. They were impressed
With gifts and cash I brought. They squashed inside
A two room flat hardships that they couldn't hide.

'I could see how stressed they were, a struggle
To keep healthy – doctors' fees. Their pay
Was small. My Polish mother Anya juggled
Shifts, though she was old, cooking in a café.
My sister Danka lived there having run away
From married life. Hard pressed but they didn't miss
Her husband who was handy with his fists.

'They always made me welcome and cooked
Me tasty foods, *pierogi*, *nalesniki*, stews
With gathered mushrooms, butter on rye bread,
Berries bought from peasant women who
Were like *babushkas* in the fairy stories.
I was entranced. This small hard working woman
Was my source, the womb I'd come from.

'She told me all the stories of our kindred
Some who died in gulags, some survived
By being Party members, some had fled
To England, some had joined the protests, strived
For *glasnost*. Now she wanted just to live
Her life, not get upset at politics
Or want revenge on corrupt communists.

'Thank God I knew her for a little while.
I had her for five years before she passed
Away. Sad, she couldn't know my past, the mile
Stones of my school and student days, best
Years of my youth, the girls I'd loved, I confessed
My wildness. She wanted to forget the years
Of war. When she talked I saw the bitter tears.

'The upset and the sense that no amount
Of time would root me so I could belong
To relatives in Poland made me doubt
My sense of self. I really wasn't strong
Enough and followed down a crazy long
And foolish route in drink – getting pissed
As if this would restore the life I'd missed.

'I crashed my car when drunk and nearly died
And lying in the hospital I thought
About self pity, wasted years and cried.
There are others where their fate has wrought
More painful, wretched lives and I sought
To change my ways – to open up my eyes
How life is full of beauty and surprise.'

All are silent when his story ends.
Though empathy is not their special gift
They admire the way that he has mended
Himself. 'Well done that you have shared but if
We all speak thus we'll have a weeping bus,'
Says Ben. 'But better if we tell the truth
Such moving tales uplift us,' argues Ruth.

We set off on our journey. Porters stack
The luggage high upon the bus. We slide
Into our seats and scan the city at our back
As the driver dodges donkeys that ride
Along the road, motorcycles, taxis, bikes.
We cross a crowded bridge. 'Is that the sea?'
Asks Ben. 'What? That's the Niger of Mali!'

I wonder if he's looked up anything at all
For this journey where we cross the ancient
Songhai Empire lands, the routes of the Sahel.
Hambo turns the air on through the vents
And we'll shut the windows if we've any sense
As clouds of red dust wrap and choke
Like the drying of tilapia with smoke.

'Well I've a comic story I could tell,'
Says Jasmine putting on her tinted lip
Salve and a dab of Dior rouge as well.
'On the GNER – a business trip,
A gentleman invited me to share a nip
Of Stolnychia. I knew he must be Russian.
I took the glass and turned on the ignition.

'We chatted for an hour or so on art
And shows – I clocked his jagged features
And his watch. His lap top was state of art.
The texture of his suit was nap of peaches.
His thoughts owed less to Marx than to Nietzsche.
Something in the diplomatic service
Which operated like a three ring circus.

'We gave our numbers when the train reached York.
He'd like to take me out to eat, he said.
I told him I was there to do arts work.
I'd meet him back in London once I'd fled
The Northern wastes. I think he had a wicked
Smile. He took my hand to say adieu and kissed
It. We'd meet in Soho for a Russian tryst.

'But when I reached my Hilton hotel bed
Expenses paid – cocktails on the house –
I realised I'd got his suitcase instead
Of mine. Same shape and strap and shade of cow.
I called his number but no answer came. Now
What to do? Curious I opened up his bag
And buggeroo what a shock I had!

'Among the shirts and underpants from best
Shops were huge high heels and sparkly evening
Dresses, loads of actor's make up, rouge, pressed
Powder, thick foundation, dangly earrings,
Strings of beads, padded bras, magic pants, things
You know cross dressers would probably adore
But to real girls scream tranny whore.

'What have we here I wondered to myself
I'll bet he wouldn't want the diplomatic
World to know that he, so skilled in stealth,
Had a sordid secret life; he got his kicks
From clubbing as an over made up minx.
There might be some advantage to me here
That will help me in my burgeoning career.

'When finally I pinned him on his phone
He joked about the mix up in a flirty
Way. "You'll want your suitcase back," I droned.
"Have you opened it?" He started sounding shirty,
So I said, "It's really not my thing how dirty
Someone gets in what they like but I'll bet
This would be shocking to ex-soviets."

'"Be careful girl you don't know how things
Operate in Russia. We don't play to rules
And I've got dark connections, can pull strings.
This isn't gossip in the yard at school."
"Oh sweetheart you're not talking to a fool.
I don't want jewels, or cash, just a chance
To be a player in the international dance.

"Invite me to the Russian embassy
I'll be the one who starts to make a profile
In exchanging artists – so you'll see
I'll make my name as someone who can nail
Elusive figures down. This will rile
My rivals. What turns you on is up to you,
In UK there are really no taboos."

'And thus began my sparkling reputation
Celebrated in the media and admired
To break down barriers across the nations
Mix up ideas and light creative fires,
Success and now I seem to be required
Presence on those TV shows about the arts.
I'm hip and their presenters are old farts.'

'It's shocking you exploited someone's secrets
To make your name. Did you have no qualms
Of conscience?' It seems that Martin felt
A little queasy at the cool and chilly calm
Of her account. 'I didn't cause him harm.
For all I know he's had his gender fixed
And now enjoys his over-made up kicks.'

Part III

The bus now slows to cross a road block,
A gendarme sleeping on a chair. His rifle rests
Across his shirt. Another slackly checks
The driver. We're tourists from the West
And unlikely to be Quaida suspects.
Kidnapping makes it harder to insure
But adds a frisson of excitement to the tour.

When the bus stops moving kids rush to sell
From trays of guavas, peanuts, skewers
Of meat, eggs, apples, mangoes; truth to tell
No-one buys food cooked by open sewers
Or the frozen ginger water – its source unsure.
Instead we take our cameras out and snap
Trays balancing on cotton head-tied wrap.

'Listen' says Martin. 'I had a glitzy job in PR,
A house in Chipping Norton, cool life style,
Just a clever boy following his star
Away from simple roots, a much-loved child,
A decent Mum and Dad, hard-working, guile-
Less whose life was home and caravan,
Allotment, TV, vaguely Anglican.

'Work hard, play hard, I travelled in my role
Promoting fizzy drinks. Charm and wit
Helped me getting on. My portfolio
And role increased. They sent me to unknit
Problems in factories abroad. The drink
Must be drunk. People must be enticed
By a cocktail of chemicals on ice.

'My love life was a circle of fire.
The gay world welcomed me – clean limbed and smart -
When I'd accepted that my sexual desire
Was not switched on by women, or heart.
I was drawn to the privileged. I aspired
To emulate their sureness of the right
To own, consume and dress as sybarite.

'But one day while working in Nepal
I visited a market to admire
The piles of harvest produce on the stalls.
I saw a woman, thin and old, bent like wire,
Pick up a small potato, hold it and enquire
About the price – a few rupees. She lay
It back, looked down and sadly walked away.

'My mother was still living at this time
And I felt how it would be if that was her
Standing hungry in the face of harvest time
And there seemed a huge abyss, unfair
Unjust, skewed by politics in the world.
Trade is warped in favour of the rich
The Goddess profit is a callous bitch.

'Once I saw a small boy begging in the snow
And ice in Leningrad – no hat or gloves -
His face was pinched – grey with misery and cold.
I was going to Tretyakov so rushed past
To meet a date – one of the new rich brats.
What did I know of living on the streets
Staying in The Emerald, champagne en-suite?

'I went back and pulled my leather gloves off
And my Berghaus hat and pressed them in his hands.
He shook, recoiled as if a Molotov
Were given as a gift, didn't understand.
A blessing from my mouth like contraband.
I smiled. Where did that come from? He grinned.
I felt good too. This has got to be win win.

'Just where does altruism come from?
It's not survival of the tribe. And a thirst
For justice, truth? The questions were a hum
A tintinnitis in my ears, but first
I had to trawl through all the answers – immerse
Myself in Tao and Testament, in Hindu
Thought, Buddhism, synagogue and voodoo.'

'Goodness,' says Jasmine 'this is growing dense.
Don't you have a lighter story, an affair
That turned hilarious? You're making us tense.
We're here to enjoy the ride, not bare
Our souls, if we have any – life's not fair.
Suck the juice from kumquats that you're given,
Useless to wonder if you can be shriven.'

'Give the man his space,' says Lee. 'I've never
Met a vicar quite like him before.
It's quite a story how he found himself.' 'Whatever,
What rubbish!' Adds Chris munching on her store
Of sweets. 'Pilgrimages! What a bore!
Like an undergrad who's just discovered Marx
At least that's rational. This is arse.'

'So are you here to think about Islam?'
Asks Ben. 'Timbuktu was a holy place,'
Says Martin. 'Scholars rode in caravans
Across the desert, pilgrims to praise
God and his Prophet.' 'And also trade,'
Says Mike 'In ivory and salt and gold
While many captured slaves were bought and sold.'

Inez smiles, 'I'm more laid back than you.
Brought up a Catholic, I know the rituals,
The Mass, the welding of ancient and new.
I go to church for marriages and funerals
But the rules are hard where the sexual's
Concerned but yes in church I kneel to pray,
Confess my failings gently – *toujours gai*!'

'A Catholic! I can't believe it, Inez,
I want to marry you but I'm an atheist
Although Jewish by descent,' Rick says.
'I can't marry someone who's delusionist
Who even sometimes takes the Eucharist.
It's sinister this clerical cabal.
How can you think they've anything at all?'

'Ah love,' says Martin. 'Why I really took
This costly trip is just like some of you,
I want a partner.' Mike shifts back a foot.
'I might surprise my parish if I had a date or two.
They'd be watching for my horns and cloven hooves
So I suppress the sexual side of me
But far from home could ease my chastity.'

Then Inez speaks, addressing all the bus,
'We've driven far and now we're close to Djenne.
We stop here for the night and time for us
To eat and in the day we'll see the women's
Co-op where they weave the famous *bogolan*,
Cloth where dyes from mud and herbs are patterned
Into abstract shapes on the home grown cotton.

Then after that we'll photograph the mosque,
A miracle in mud-brick, forty metres high,
A fluid, patterned shape. You can ask
The guide how old it is. It all defies
Belief. Gaudi learned from buildings such as these.
Then the market after that to look for masks,
Cloth, carvings, baskets, other artefacts.'

Part IV

Over eggs and tea we meet our Dogon man
Koguem who'll be our guide and cook
Along the journey. He is a village man,
A Dogon, an elder, and he really looks
The part in homespun village cloth, but ruck
Sack from Nike and Timberland boots,
A mix of fashion from the West and roots.

Although he never went to school he speaks
French and bits of English too. He is
Strong from ranging up and down the peaks
And cliffs in Dogon country where he also has his
Fields to farm – millet, onions, goats – they subsist
On those but what he earns from working as a guide
Pays school fees and the scooter that he rides.

He is courteous, calm and ever charming.
We are adjectival to his subject noun.
He clearly sees the way we are alarming;
When things are just a little late we frown,
Ridicule each other with put downs,
Our bickering and selfishness expressed
I want the seat and food and tent that's best.

The mosque of course is stunning. We stare
And photograph. Fateha can go inside
So dons a scarf and covers up her long dark hair
To enter. Respectfully she joins the prayers
But the Imam calls her to an office at the side.
He's sick and wants to know if she can make
Him well. He's coughing and his body shakes.

She checks out pulse and chest as best she can so
Advises him to rest and drink more milk
And laughs about her diagnosis as we go
To market. 'I don't think he's really sick
Just a chest infection. Men get on your wick.
Such drama. Surely if he's spiritual
He'll think he's bound for heaven not for hell.'

She buys some blankets from the women's stall
And makes a bargain – then onto stores of wood,
Window shutters, locks and masks. They're all
From Dogon villages, hand carved. 'Hey, should
You take these out the country? Such wood
Is scarce,' says Ursula who's bought a ring
Of raised red stone and other Songhai bling.

Fateha just sighs. 'It's honest money earned
For carvers. I'm sure they can make more.
These windows aren't antique or rare.
It's recent work. The villagers are poor.
They'd rather feed and clothe themselves before
They're given charity and loans and aid.
They want to farm and work and get stuff paid.'

'You're right,' says Rick, 'I can't see why we give
Handouts to a bunch of corrupt, failing states.
It's swallowed by the ruling class. The rest live
As they've always done. No gold-plated
Limousines or palaces for them! What a waste!
My grandparents were immigrants with zilch.
Through effort, cunning, thrift we finished rich.'

When sunset falls the group sit down to drink
Some beer. Ruth wears her wax-cloth gown
With head-tie. She dances to the music –
Wouya orchestra with *balafon*
And drums, *ngoni*. The singer is a woman,
A *djelimuso* with deep, powerful grace.
The audience tuck money in her waist.

After chips and chicken in the campement
The bus chugs off to reach the area
Where the Dogon live: the Escarpement
But first stop is the central town of Sangha
A cocktail of poverty and filth, a mecca
For the restless drifted there in search of bucks
And latest stuff, a culture in a state of flux.

In this dry place we stay in a hotel
With showers and electricity all day,
Child prostitutes at the gate. One little
Girl approaches Lee. He brushes her away
Shaken and upset. 'She's young enough to play
With dolls,' he tells Finn. The side effects
Of tourists coming here – perverted sex.

The trek begins, the heat intense.
We cool off under Baobab trees, pull water
From the wells and drop in iodine in case.
We smell jasmine and hear children's laughter.
Our stuff is carried by a string of porters.
The witches' hat-shaped granaries bring charm
And we're impressed by thriving onion farms.

From there we walk across and down the cliffs
Along the winding, ancient tracks past caves,
Once ancient tombs. The hieroglyphs
Of villages are written on the land. Waves
Of savannah stretch out like parched lava.
We eat and camp by kerosene filled lights
And listen to the village in a star-filled night.

Because Renee and Jasmine will not share
'There's no tent left for Koguem,' Inez
Points out. 'Why should he sleep outside? It's not fair.
Can't you see your selfishness?' she says.
'This trip cost dosh – I really couldn't care.
That's it, I'm off to sleep,' replies our Jasmine.
'Mmm,' says Renee and bats her eyes at him.

Ben looks at Inez shakes his head and talks.
'Is there something in the water on this trip?
Jay and Ruth romancing on a moonlit walk
And Koguem is not averse to plastic hips.'
'Predatory cow.' Inez screws up her pretty lips.
'And you could marry this our lawyer guest
And live a life of luxury in Key West.'

....

'They live an Iron Age life,' says Renee
'Not interesting to me. I miss
The architecture and the history
Of Bambara and Songhai culture.' 'Why diss
The Dogon people?' Ruth frowns. 'They subsist
On what they grow and trade. It's ancient too
Older than the Muslim world of Timbuktu.

Look how little water here is used
To grow crops, breed goats, keep clean.'
'Hey,' says Rick. 'They want the stuff that we abuse.
You think they don't want smart machines,
Cars, houses, fridges, flat TV screens?
Or hospitals or surgeons or midwives,
Flush toilets too? Hey Ruth. Get a life.'

Part V

'Has no-one got a story' says Ben 'that will
Pass the time?' 'There's something I could tell
A queer and haunting story,' says Lee.
'I'm from a mining village near Peterlee
And my father was a miner, as was his
Before him. But if you go beyond this
You find an Irish immigrant who fled
Hunger, came in search of work and bread.
We're called left-footers but don't practise –
Work and pub and football will suffice.
But the mine was closed. My Dad with time
To spare watched porn and horror films
At home – zombies, devils, vampires –
Films people use to kill the empty hours.
My sister likes a drink but wasn't pissed
When she told us she'd begun to notice
Things moving by themselves like plates
Bowls, spoons were flying through the air and wait,
The hoover cleaned up, the toilet flushed
When no-one was at home. The lights flashed
On and off. The music centre blasted out
Loud rock. Dad ran to see what's wrong.
She'd bleached just like a double sheet that's hung
Out in the sunshine. At first we took it
As a joke until we stayed at home to wit-
ness strange and weird phenomenon.
We felt as though the house was full of demons.
Dad went to the police and asked a constable
To call and witness how the chairs and tables
Lifted of themselves. "You want me to arrest
The spirit do you for being such a pest?
Disturbance of the peace. We'll do his DNA
And see if he has previous. What'd you say?"
"At least come round and look," my father asked.
"Ok," he said "I'll call the next time when I pass"
And so he did. The hoover zoomed upstairs;
A plate flew by his head. The copper stared

And ran right out the house. "You'll never see
Me back," he trembled "not for all the tea
In China." Well we were stumped and terrified
Of living in the house but no-where else to hide.
"I'm going to fetch the priest," I said,
"Even if I have to get him from his bed.

"I think he might forgive and understand
We're lazy sinful folk. Anyway I'm damned
If I can think of owt else to do. I'll beg him
Bring a blessing, prayer or holy hymn
To drive these fiendish spirits from the place.
Yeah, the last time we visited a church was
When my sister Jordan was baptised
But he'll have to help us." I rang his bell
Until he opened, rubbed his eyes, and, "Well,"
He said, "What unearthly time is this my lad?"
"No time at all I'm sorry Father, don't be mad,
We want you now to come and bless our home.
Bring holy water, crucifix and oil from Rome
To exorcise. We seem to be possessed
By demons – most unwelcome guests."
"Do I know you family?" " No I'm sorry we don't
Go to church but now this spirit's come to haunt
Us it's made us think of angels and devils
Once again. It feels like there's an evil
Presence there, though we're just ordinary
People." He agreed to come and prayed
In every room. He blessed the house while
We stayed in the cold outside – terrified.
We asked if he would stay there for some hours
To be sure and he did. He was generous
With his time. After that the spirits eased off
Their interference just occasionally stuff
Seemed to shift but perhaps it was our fear.
This made me think. Once I saw a bonfire
In the woods, people dancing. I hacked
Along the ground and saw they all were naked
Dancing in a circle round a dog staked
To the ground. A twig beneath me cracked

And one man picked a flaming band to check
The ground for prowlers. His face was furious
So I shimmied back into the bushes
Really scared by what I'd seen. Something dark
Was happening – it wasn't just a silly lark.'
'Nothing harmful, surely with these ancient
Rites,' says Martin. 'We must respect; it's meant
In praise of mother earth, with her cycles
Of death and life. Don't let minor niggles
About monotheism prejudice us
Against those who sacrifice to worship thus.'
'Well I'm not an educated man,' says Lee.
'I see what kindness does for me.
There's more to life than pub and sport
And chasing skirt. There's doing what you ought.'

As we trek between the curious Dogon
Villages, the thud of pestle and mortar
Pounding sorghum – kids begging *bic et bonbon*
We near the town of Bandiaraga.
We ask a story of our poet Ursula.
She unpins her long red hair and lets it down
And lowers her plump backside to the ground.

We settle by a stream with lilies floating,
And wash our dusty feet within its coolness.
Koguem shows us recent fox prints, noting
Their sequence and pattern, making sense
Of their predictions. Ursula's impressed.
'He has such quiet dignity,' she says.
'You're not planning husband four?' enquires Inez.

'No three's enough, when young the first was Greek,
The next Jamaican, the third is from Iraq.
The first was a drummer; in three fierce weeks
I'd married him, his hands as rough as bark
But fire cools, and tired of lying in the sack
I watched as poverty began to stalk
Us, callous as a focussed hungry hawk.

'At thirty three and trying to make a name
As poet I met another wannabee
Like me, whose goal was monetary fame.
He performed dub in patois. I didn't see
The way he stalked my contacts and used me
To get his name electric, just a prelude
To be the *Guardian* readers' coolest dude.

He found another woman poet higher
In esteem that me and hit on her.
I think they're still together; his writing's dire,
Predictable and clichéd. No-one cares.
He gets away with it because he's debonair,
Unscrupulous and cunning as the KGB
I could cheerfully have melted him to gee.'

'So is number three a poet too?' asks Dieter.
'God no!' she laughs and eats her sandwich.
'He fled here from the war, an asylum seeker.
Tariq's a sweetie from Baghdad. I've hitched
Myself to him so he has rights to stay.
If I tell you what's afoot – don't be enraged.
My pretty man is only half my age.'

He's got a place for a degree in law.
He dreams he'll help the poor, the dispossessed,
So clever, working hard and what's more
He's beautiful, in spirit too, honest
And spiritual. His prayer-mat's pressed
Against the floor 5 times a day, South East
To Mecca. Will wonders ever cease?

'So why've you left behind this paragon?'
Asks Renee, who disapproves of girls
Who let themselves get plump – this ton
Of lard, she mutters, with a bulging girth
She ought to cover with a flapping shirt.
'The novel that I'm writing's based on just
The kind of thing that's happening on this bus.'

Embarrassed by this frankness, open faced
And blue-eyed gaze, the dusty tourists turn
To getting up their tents and washing face
And hands in bottled water, cream on sunburn,
Seeing if they have a signal. The porters earn
Their keep unfolding tables, setting plates
And making sure the dinner isn't late.

We buy a goat – the porters kill and roast
It on a wooden spit. Now I know why
Goat is missing off most menus. It's almost
Impossible to chew. The village try
To be good hosts and send out twenty
Girls to dance for us. The porters hit
The pans to get a rhythm for their feet.

When we've eaten plenty goat enough
And Dieter's swigged the champagne in his case
We join the dancing – at least the laughs
Are plenty and no-one loses face
When the meat we didn't eat is taken off
By villagers and shared around. 'Well,'
Says Jay, 'You all look tired. I have a tale to tell.

From when I was sixteen I had a need
For risk – face danger and not lose my cool.
I rode a motorbike at typhoon speeds
To London from my home in Hartlepool.
The army tamed me, taught me self-control.
There wasn't much of that where I came from –
Wild brothers and an often pissed up Mum.'

'You must,' says Ruth 'have seen a few things
In your time.' Jay tips his cap from off his face
And sees the pretty smile, the silver earrings
In the amber ears, the narrow waist.
'This limp,' says he 'is from a mine. By grace
Of God or I'd be legless. I fought against
The Argies in the Falklands, what a waste!
More sheep than people in the friggin' place.'

'A squaddie then,' says Chris, lip curled.
'I don't agree with countries using power
To crush civilians in the far flung world
Who once were colonised, oppressed and poor.
I'm a pacifist. Destroy all nuclear
Weapons. Why choose a job that lets you kill?
Do you get off on this? Are these cheap thrills?'

'What d'you know of what a bloke like me would feel
Or why we'd choose the army and enlist
To make a life? You've never lacked a meal.
What gives you the right to sneer and diss
Lads like me? On little pay we take our risks
For what you can't unknot or quite pin down,
A green, kind land – not government or crown.

'Sometimes we know who the baddies are.
In Freetown the fighting was with vicious guys
Who'd brutalized poor children in their war
On decent life – cold faces, hearts of ice,
Dressed like dudes, wearing new bazookas.
With a trail of brown-brown and cocaine
'Trained small boys in ways of causing pain.'

'So yes, I was a paid up soldier – a squaddie
Been in Ireland and the Red Sea Gulf
Like many lads from mean streets and cities
Rough around the edges. Schooling? Not much.
Petty crime, drunken brawling, drugs n stuff.
We couldn't know the reason for such anger
The English in Ireland, the Great Hunger.

'We were there to keep the bleedin' peace.
Stop blokes intent on murdering Catholics
Or Prods – blokes like us who went out on the piss.
They both believe in Jesus on the Crucifix.
It's barmy – but we were targets for the Micks.
What happened to turned cheek of Christian love?
St. Michael must be grinding teeth above.

'It was messier in the Gulf War and Iraq.
What? If they grew sprouts instead of oil
No way we Brits or even richer Yanks
Would fight across that burnt out soil.
It's obvious it was CH23 spoils.
I watched out for my mates, did my best
Not think of politics and all the dirty rest.

'Now I run a lorry business – across
The EEC. At least the army taught me
How to drive long distance. Turned me from toss
Pot into citizen! My brothers and me
We had no discipline. Our mum, you see,
Was abandoned by our Dad. She tried
To get us right but her spirit died.'

'Shall we watch your temper while we're cramped
In this our 4 X 4,' says Jasmine 'it seems
You flood when stormy waters fill your dam.'
Jay laughs. 'It's good to let off steam
When things aren't right – see what I mean?
In Freetown I almost shot a man, why?
He stole a sandwich I'd given to a child.

'When we sailed from Plymouth south along
The Atlantic swell to Sierra Leone
It was a good thing sorting right from wrong.
The blue-mountained coast, the spill of foam
On palm-fringed beach, the unknown
City spilt across hills. It was strangely dark.
Electricity was cut. We waited to embark.

'We were warned the soldiers and the rebels
Were in cahoots – had turned on the city
And its people, burning, looting, rape – a hell
On earth. Children abducted without pity,
Feet and hands chopped off with a machete,
Things perverse too that made us shiver
A mother made to eat her shot son's liver.

'Our regiment was sent to drive these sons
Of bitches out of town but the Nigerians
Did more in hand to hand and gun to gun
Fighting, with many losses in the intense
Battles to push them back – their Alpha jets
Heartened and scared people to their knees
With prayers for this to end and bring back peace.

'We were focused on small operations
Mopping up the random rebel gangs.
People were hungry and we had rations.
One thin boy pulled my sleeve. Sarge harangued
Him for hassling us. He pointed to his tongue
To show his hunger, and said, "I beg you please."
I gave him chocolate, bread and cheese.

'As we walked away I saw an adult push
The boy and send him flying, then snatch
The food and cram it in his mouth and woosh
It down. I was incensed, pulled back the catch
And pointed it ready to dispatch
This bastard. I aimed it at his shining head.
"Give back the food or you'll be lying dead."

'This desperate, hungry man. If he robbed
A child again I'd kill him – no sweat.
A sandwich. A tiny moment of job
Justice. Who knows if that boy ever ate
Again. Or the man. It's down to fate.
We went home. Life goes on. People survive
Or not. Everything wants to stay alive.

'How did you really get your limp?' asks Ruth.
'Yeah I said it was defusing mines
Or I could say saving wounded mates. The truth
Is what I want to give you. How I unwind
Is speed, fresh air and a well designed
Machine.' 'Not a motor-bike! That's rich!
Mid-life men can be so easily bewitched.'

'An accident in Weardale on a road
That beautifully rises, curves and dips.
I looked across the moors and peaks and slowed
But hit a lamb. Me and the bike pitched
Into a wall and bracken-feathered ditch.
After all the fire fights in such troubled spots
To have my ankles smashed by English rocks!'

Part VI

Our trek in Dogon land is done. Porters stash
Our luggage in the bus. A scramble for the seats.
Lee rolls tobacco in his papers with some hash
He's bought in Dougo. He offers Jay his neat
Concoction. Jay grins and takes. 'Oh sweet!'
The memory of Dogon people disappears
Like dawn mist rising in the atmosphere.

'Enough,' says Ben 'we're here at the hotel
In Mopti.' He wipes some red dust off his face.
'We'll have a meal of Niger perch as well
As beer. You all consume it by the case!
We'll later walk to port for our *pinasse*
That takes us up the Niger, with our crew
On the five day sail to Timbuktu.'

We see the huge fish on a slab of wood
Macheted into cutlets by the chef
Then fried in sauce – by heck its flavour's good.
A band comes out. You'd have to be tone deaf
Not to let your spirits lift with such a deft
Weave of grace notes from the djelimuso
Her voice andante then furioso.

Malians put notes in her skirt or on
Her sweating forehead. She sings as if the world
Was going to end – *cri de coeur* strong
And rich. She stops and then a man curled
In a corner drags his polio-withered
Legs upon the stage and starts to sing
His raw voice pierced with melancholy longing.

Ruth gets up and dances just a turn
From hip to hip. She swings her bubu gown.
Jay watches mesmerised. His heart burns.
She holds up one side of her dress and round
Her head she's tied a piece of cotton like a crown
With wings. Her shoulders weave a shape of eight.
Jay wonders could she ever be his mate.

Chris complains because there's no en-suite.
She purses at the onions on her plate.
Lee goes off to make some rollies tight and neat
And offers them to the porters who wait
Until the kitchen's done with us. As mates
They'll share and eat with fingers from one dish
Of rice and spicy sauce, a little fish.

When the music stops there's thickening silence
In the group. They have no wish to hear
How each are feeling. Why such pretence
When you've paid a lot to travel here?
Just make sure you're given your full share
Of guides, rooms, food, tours, the whole caboodle
So you can boast to colleagues while they doodle.

Ursula walks to Mopti's river side
Where *pinasses*, painted in bright gloss
Jostle against the market stalls – tie-dye
And wax cloth stacked in bales, hawkers and chaos,
Peppers, yams, onions, okra, strewn across
The pavements; striped plastic kettles, fans, mats,
Charcoal burners, tin bowls, pointed straw hats.

Thirst takes her to a bar by the river-side.
She opens Chaucer, reads *The Wife of Bath*.
The Castel chills her heated up insides.
The prologue with its payoff makes her laugh.
People are people, pensioner or youth.
We're devious and dreaming, kindness and threat.
What you see is never what you get.

The best seat in the boat is not the back
Where the hole for toilet is, and the fumes
Of diesel waft the air – Chris attacks
The queue to board, elbowing with awesome
Force. Not dead in front – the optimum
Seats are two thirds up – the wind is rather chill
And too much sun will leave you feeling ill.

'She should watch herself,' says Jay to Mike
'Rough justice is the norm where I abide.'
'Is this post feminism or something like?'
The latter wonders. 'She reminds me of the pike
I fish for in the ponds of England's countryside.
Even money launderers behave with grace
Arrange assassinations without haste.'

As the *pinasse* chugs along the slow
Green river Niger, thickets of acacia trees
Rustle by the banks where villages grow
And shrink with Saharan sand. Beyond we
See the endless desert, the tyranny
Of sun and space. Finn stretches lengthwise
His huge frame atop the cabin, and sighs.

Tony opens up the case of his binoculars
And scans for hoopoes, cranes and firebirds
As the water wallows by, for night jars
And herons. He's lost for human words
As focused through the glass the world
Of nature fills his inward turning mind
Unaware of others' needs but not unkind.

'Water reminds me of how I found my wife,'
Finn says, 'a Buddhist since I left the Church
Though sometimes visions of the after-life
Haunted me, fear of Hell, but I searched
For simpler truths to live by and lurched
From Pentecostalist to Rasta
And its holy smoke, misogynist disaster.

'It's the gentle side of Buddhism that attracts,
Teaches me to live a simpler way,
Not stress out on ecclesiastics.
I like restrained emotion – the inner gaze
Stilling my passions as I meditate
Create good Karma doing noble things
Accepting how life twists and stills and swings.

'An ascetic and a veggie take on life
Is fine to cleanse a self regarding soul
But I'm human and wanted earthly love
A woman as a wife to make me whole.'
We listen to the fiddle playing of his vowels
As his ocean eyes rest still with memories
Flowing salt and clear like tidal seas.

'I woke up one night from a dream so vivid
In which I'd met the woman I was meant
To marry. I'd travelled to an island
By boat, light singing on the rocks, wind-bent
Trees. I met a small, strong, confident
Woman with thick black hair and grey eyes.
Kittiwakes around us swooped and cried.

'In the dream I saw her not lonely, but alone
In a white-washed cottage. She fetched water
From a pump. A goat grazed her overgrown
Garden. Her voice sang with low-pitched laughter
Like a cello playing vibrato. I took her
Hand and knew. What island? Was it Aran
Or Achill, somewhere windswept barren?

'Blasket's lost its people – but had she
Gone to live there like a hermit from the past?
Or was she in an artists' colony? Beads
And bits of glass, twinkled, weavings fast-
Ened to the walls. My imagination raced.
I'd search for somewhere isolated
Where Atlantic sunsets radiated.

'I travelled when I'd time a year or more
But cottages I found were empty, wrecked.
The Cork road took me west to Baltimore
Where ferries bellied tourists on the deck
To visit Shearkin and Cape Clear, like sects
Of pilgrims with their staffs and sacks
Upon expensive Gorex cladded backs.

'Clear? My heart leapt at the simple word.
The light was piercing. I saw each petal
Of the fuchsia hedges waving seaward,
Each frill of foam upon the emerald
Waves. As the boat swung my heart trembled.
We passed the gentle curves of Shearkin
And the waves summoned massive Finn.

'The island's bleak in winter – in strong
Storms no boats for days. Those who live there
Have old ways, story-telling and tribal songs.
The men are over six feet tall, like me. Clear
Island has its own race in that ocean frontier.
A place of old beliefs and gentler ways
Where centuries are folded into days.

'I walked around the island when we docked,
Went into both the pubs and downed a dram
For courage. A peat fire burned. I looked
Around hoping my lovely aisling came
To find me. But no. I dashed the road that framed
This ancient place, thrown by the Gods
From Cork, once rich from fishing cod.

'Berries shone like onyx in the hedges, aflame
With monbretia, scented honeysuckle,
Toad flax, thrift, fox-glove and wild thyme.
A woman passed me on her bicycle,
Her basket full of flowers – "Oh miracle!"
I cried. She stared as if I were a lunatic
But love was bubbling in my bloodstream.
This was the woman shown me in my dream.

'My size and big grin made it worse. She pedalled
Like a steam train round the brambled bend.
I ran with arms outstretched – she skidaddled
Down a pebbled lane. I tripped and ended
In a muddy ditch. Now I'd offended
Perhaps the very one – not shown what soul
Lay smouldering in this human bean-pole.

'I looked down the lane and there below
I saw the cottage of my psychic dream.
The door was red, the walls limed white as snow.
She turned her long dark head of hair and screamed
When she saw me as if I was a demon
So I backed off and then returned to base
To think of other strategies and ways.

'I sent bouquets and letters to entice
Her for a meal – I explained my search
And how a dream began it all. She was wise
To know I couldn't be a dramaturge
And if a blackguard I'd have used more subterfuge.
She met me for a meal and watched me clear-
Eyed across the table. At last I had her near.

'We told our stories in the hotel bar
Then walked beside the ocean in the night
Scattered with a million brilliant stars
That flickered green and yellow in such air
And the ocean glittered black as fresh laid tar.
What to do? She had another suitor;
Besiege with gifts I'd order on computer.

'I sent one ringhorn hen, two snowwhite ducks,
Three sugar mice, four paisley silken stoles,
Five bars of honey soap, six travel books,
Seven scented candles, eight white towels,
Nine plum and apple trees, ten bags of coal
Delivered by the boat from Baltimore.
How could she thus my overtures ignore?'

'Such a romantic tale.' Inez essayed.
'Where I come from men nod you up to dance
Buy you a short and think they've paid
To spend the night with you – their hands
Are everywhere before you've left, their fangs
Are on your throat. One-night stands!
They think I'll lie back on their sweaty sheets
As if they'd bought a joint of roasted meat.

'I want someone who'll woo me, understand
And love me for my soul not because I'm
Tanned and toned, with tiny feet and hands.
To show me off they'll hang me from their arm
But would they fight to keep me safe from harm?
How to find a man who'll keep his marriage vow
And stick to one he's courted here and now?'

'Have faith,' says Finn and lays hands on her head.
'Listen to your instincts. Don't fall for dross
Because it shines – look for carat gold instead.
Take your time – hold back – find out what his ethos
And his dreams are. A lovely girl supposes
That if a man's made love to you in bed
That he means all the pretty words he's said.'

'Inez,' Rick lifts his hand, 'you want a husband?
There's me! I'll take you to the sunshine state.
I'm a lawyer – good at it. Folk demand
I take their cases. I own prime real estate
With private beach. We could even procreate!'
Her liquorice eyes are rolled up to the stars.
'You? Your politics are coming out your arse.'

The pinasse chugs through Niger's green slow water.
Kingfishers dive and hawks soar across
The sand. A fisherman with perch to barter
Holds up two silver bodies. The boats jostle
One on one like two rhinoceros,
Koguem talks price in words like drums along
The river, the rhythms of an ancient tongue.

Part VII

Lunch-time on the river Niger – the cook
Stands ankle deep in water with his pots.
He hands on plates to Finn who drops his book
And passes on the food. 'This isn't hot!'
Snarls Chris but keeps it where she's sat
And will not pass a cup or plate to others
Sat beyond her. She can't be bothered.

'I'm not full of the milk of human kindness,'
Says Rick 'but we need to hand stuff down.
What's your problem? Don't you do politeness?'
'Oh shut your bourgeois mouth,' she frowns.
'This is ridiculous,' adds Inez. 'Pass it down.'
'Why should I lift a finger for such as you?
You're an overpaid and hedonist ragout.'

'Are you a communist?' ask Mike and Rick
'We should've known.' 'I'm not,' she says aggrieved.
'They're compromised – too many stupid dicks
With bleeding hearts on their organic sleeves.
Ruthless power! All else is make believe.
No change unless the gutters run with red.
Destroy the slimy status quo instead.'

'Oh you're revolutionary party?'
Jasmine rolls her eyes. 'How very quaint.'
'You parallel,' says Rick 'the Tea Party.
You're both noxious and feather-brained.
See this squalor. Let capitalism remain!'
'She's not active any more.' Tony speaks
Seeing his companions bare their teeth.

'That's the first thing I have heard you say,'
Martin smiles. 'I've seen you brush your partner's hair
When we had picnics on the Dogon way
And help her when she pushed us out the way
To get first on the bus – you're a devoted pair.'
'Fifteen years ago we met on picket lines.
Bye! I thought, here's a woman knows her mind.

'She's done well at work – runs her department
Like a naval ship – lazy councillors in tow.
If she banished all the tennis courts in Kent
They wouldn't blink – the secrets that she knows!
Secret figures in accounts, some stuff on video.'
'But have you two got any friends?' Ruth glares.
'Friends?' Chris laughs 'What for? Who cares?'

'*Yes,*' says Mike. 'I've listened to you rabbit on.
The savannah as a backdrop, dust and heat
Beyond the tussocks, turbaned herdsmen
Striding with their flocks of goats. It's a treat
To get to know this motley crew of sweet
And sour. You think I've nothing much to say
Just the finger on the Cannon clicks all day.

'It's true that taking photographs is art
To me an East End boy who grew up tough.
I haven't got much time for pompous farts
Who stink of privilege. I'm just a bit of rough
To them – a lucky oik who's learned to bluff
And useful too – I dole out cash for shows
Of art, poncy stuff for those who're in the know.

'Yeah, I have 2 million pounds of Regency
A white-washed terrace house; a garden
Cooled by larch and black tree fern – privacy
Like all good things costs. Making it hardens
You but I've got good taste in women.
My trophy wife's an Asian babe, a smart hostess.
Her beauty, Nefertiti-like Goddess.

'Educated in the best not with riffraff.
Her father thought I was a bit of muck.
He's big in steel but small in paying staff.
He appreciates that I'm as smart as fuck
At keeping Madhi in her nip n tuck
And Jimmy Choos, Armani and some Prada
Thus dousing any instinct for palaver.

'I began with houses in the Isle of Dogs,
Stepney, Wapping and Mile End, those blighted
Boroughs. My tenants were immigrants, wogs,
The Cockneys called them. They weren't delighted
With my liberal business plan but frightened
To kick off – I had connections – my mates
From school were good at throwing round their weight.

'The rest is history. So here I'm bringing out
My inner artist – tasty photographs
Of mosques, turbans, topless girls wringing out
Their washing at the river side – I pay cash –
Also shining perch, markets, babies on backs.
I'll have a private show in London's South Bank,
Easy with spondula in the bank.

'You make it sound corrupt and sleazy,'
Says Jasmine who wipes her hands with dettol.
'To get a show requires a brain, it's not so easy.
Here's what I have to say. Art needs to unsettle
People's views not give them postcard pics of gentle
People in exotic spots. You can't know
What's cutting edge in stills and video.'

Mike points his lens at Jasmine's pout
In the cross hairs of the focus. 'Well I've time
Along this lazy ride for you to put
Me in the picture – I like a girl who climbs
On others gleaning riches in the harvest time.
You're twenty carat; I like your haughty style.'
Jasmine feels herself a tad beguiled.

'I couldn't give a toss for that,' says Ruth
'What bothers me is your snapping Malians –
A woman walking miles across this rough
Terrain to sell one goat to buy some grain
Captured if she's thin and beautiful enough.
In Yougo you filmed the 'sacred' ritual
We paid for – hardly something spiritual.'

'You've told us that you started life as poor,'
Jasmine's mamba smile 'how did you change your fate
To make it into property, tell us more?
Did you rob a bank or asphyxiate
A witness? Blackmail a rotten magistrate?'
Mike grins. 'I feel as though I've met my match
In you – cool as cava, knowing as a witch.'

'Let's face it: we're here because we've got cash
In our accounts – we can afford to spend
On our desires. We don't donate our stash
To orphanages or buy peasants a crash
Course in farming – or help conflict end.
It's great to go where things are really cheap.
Our Rohan pockets now feel truly deep.'

'Look, you don't know the old East End
Before the spruced up squares and swanky flats.
There are tunnels underneath the River Thames
Secret ways known just to locals and to rats,
Dripping brickwork from the dead and buried past.
As boys we'd go down for a bet or dare
Though truth to tell the shadows left us scared.

'One time, I found a man asleep, stretched out,
A blanket pulled up to his shaven pate.
My stare awoke him – his green eyes raked about
And saw a scruffy, cockney tearabout.
He leaped and seized me tightly by the throat. "What
Have we here? He said, 'Better tell no-one
What you seen here – you got that son?"

'I nodded. Where I come from you never grass.
It's in my DNA. He released his hairy grip
And smiled. I saw humour in his sallow face.
He boxed with me a little, then hands on hips
He said "I'm on the run boy. Nothing's passed my lips
For three days. Get me something good to eat.
You look smart and sharp about the feet."

'I'd been to Catholic school. I knew the teaching –
Feed the hungry – help those worse off –
Mum didn't have much in her kitchen
But I got some bread and jam and stuffed
It in my coat – grabbed a pint of milk and ran off.
She hammered me for taking food but I kept
Him fed until the time came and he left.

'I'd get letters sent from Spain and then Brazil
With dollars tucked inside on every birthday.
My mum was dumbstruck and she grilled
Me for the truth so I gave the tale away
And she spent this money from my runaway.
When I was eighteen he sent me real bread.
I could've blown it but bought property instead.'

We stop by the riverside to camp. The ground's
Sepia as the villages of mud built
Houses and streets. The sun bakes them brown
In the oven of the afternoon. We taste grit
In our green tea – the first pouring is bit –
ter like death, but the last is sweet like love
And in between the one that tastes like life.

Some boys arrive in ragged clothes, hungry
And bruised – *talibes*. They shake the cans
Around their necks for cash. Finn gets angry
At their begging for the marabout, the man
Who sends them out reeling off the Koran.
'They live like slaves – I'm sure they haven't eaten.
If they come back with nothing they'll get beaten.'

'Not all the *marabouts* are like that Finn,'
Fateha tips back the cotton sun-hat.
'There are some good ones where they take in
Orphans, boys from families without
The means to feed them. It's true that
They study the Koran, but sleep safe at night
Get fed and learn to read and write.'

'Yes Fateha maybe it's unfair of me
To damn them all. You can tell me more.
Would you take me to the mosque to see
Inside and tell me what for you's the core
Of your belief? I'd love that.' 'Are you sure?'
She smiles up at this hairy, gentle giant.
She's never met a man like Finbar Ryan.

Next day past many villages they glide,
Mud built squares of houses, a school, a mosque.
'Can we stop at one?' Rick asks the guide.
'I've got a sack of pens, pencils, rubbers, books
I'd like to give the kids – school stuff.' Ben looks
In shock but signals for the boat to land
And Rick jumps down with treasure in his hands.

When he returns our lovely guide Inez
Smiles and flashing her dark eyes holds
Out her hand to help him up and says
'That was so cool. I assumed…You never told
Us you were bringing gifts. I pigeon-holed
You for a First World even racist git.'
Rick took her hand in his and kissed the tip.

'That doesn't mean I think that Aid should go
Unquestioned,' he grins. 'Look at the waste
Of river water here. Other countries know
To make the desert bloom – ways to irrigate.
Look at Israel and its fruit estates.'
Inez drops her hand and howls. 'You see –
Too many things on which we disagree.

'They grow the food they need – sufficient rice
To keep the family. It's irrigated
In an ancient way patterned, to be precise,
On seasons known as wet and dry. They wait
For rain to make the river inundate.
That's how they grow their first-rate cotton too,
Exported from the state of Timbuktu.'

Part VIII

We see camels march across the burning sand.
They cast long shadows in late afternoon.
The shuffle of their feet's the only sound
As they carry slabs of salt across the dunes
Fanning out the miles of distance to Sudan.
We watch the Tuareg, the people of the veil,
Escort the caravan along its ancient trail.

Each bowl of water that we wash in, drains
The deep down water table that they need
To drink and cook and grow their grains
Their mango, dates and paw paw trees,
Let their donkeys, goats and camels feed.
The desert moves south – trees chopped for kindling
Nomads struggle to survive, herds dwindling.

Our tents are set up on the river side on sand.
The cook builds up a fire from gathered wood.
The silent desert stretches timeless, beyond
Our self importance, our ignorance of words
That speak its habitat, or write its wind
And stones; we wouldn't last three days, our bones
Bleached in the heat, scattered and unknown.

But the meal is ready and the table set.
We'll eat and argue whether Dogons
Really found the Sirius star or not.
There's politics and books but no-one
Talks of how our life style hits upon
The people here – how much we waste
Leaving the region worn out and debased.

Like them tonight we go behind a bush
And dig a hole to bury our fat shit
And use a jug of water for a wash
Though Ursula will strip out of her kit
To wade into the River Niger for a bit
Of coolness, for water on her sweating skin.
Bilharzias is the risk of going in.

The desert's moving south. Frequent droughts,
Overgrazing and an over-heated world
Have led to loss of habitat throughout
The Sahel. A changing way of life for nomads –
Few animals to hunt and dwindling herds
Lead to conflict or settling in towns
A cultural change uneasy and profound.

Chris gets a spade and bowl from our Inez
To go beyond the desert scrub to find
A place to wash and do her business.
Her husband with binoculars has his mind
On feathered creatures of another kind.
He doesn't see her wander off nor count
The time she's gone nor hear her distant shout.

But as the sky sprints into darkness Ben
Wonders has she eaten so much dinner
That her shit is taking on munificence
And she'll return a good deal thinner.
The sight of a rare Little Bittern
Is occupying Tony who waves away
His colleagues' faint expressions of dismay.

Ben searches out along the track she went
To see if something's wrong – maybe she fell
And broke her ankle. 'Yeah, an accident
Is likely in the desert,' Jay adds. 'Infidels
Cannot read the land.' 'Surely she would yell
If injured – the sound would echo far across
This empty space,' says Ruth. 'Do you give a toss?'

Mike waves and settles down inside his tent.
The stars are coming out – sparkling and green
The air's so pure. Renee looks ambivalent
But doesn't want to wander out between
The dunes to look for someone who isn't 'scene'.
Ursula whispers into Tony's ear
To tell him that his wife has disappeared.

Koguem is sent to follow tracks in sand
But the wind is blowing and the night's
Moon is thin – he switches on a flashlight
And sees many footprints patterning the land.
The tourists' troubled bellies led them out to shite.
He wonders if this is a place of djinns
Looks around and shivers in his skin.

He tells Inez and Ben of what he fears –
Have packs of striped hyenas hauled
Her off to chew? The others are all ears.
Have djinns seized her? The tourists are appalled.
What nonsense! They hope the journey won't be stalled
By such a contretemps – what can they do?
In two days time they must reach Timbuktu.

Tony runs from dune to dune and shouts
And uses his binoculars to look
For her familiar shape in khaki shorts.
'Perhaps she was confused and mistook
Her pathway back – or had the bad luck
To be caught by bandits – surely the police
Must now be called – Inez and Ben – please!'

'There's no way we can talk to them before
We dock in Timbuktu – no signal here.
We will report her missing to the law
And get the Embassy to bend their ear
To get policemen out to persevere
And find her. Perhaps you'll get a ransom
Message soon or text.' Tony is struck dumb.

Two more *pinasse* days and sandy nights.
The sun will set behind the desert dunes – red
And fiery. Then mauve and lemon lights
Will blonde the delta. We set up tents and beds.
Koguem fires up charcoal so we'll all be fed.
Shadows move at night from tent to tent.
Love springs up, unfeigned or fraudulent.

At Niafunke Koguem ties the *pinasse* up
Jasmine wants to see where Mali's king
Of music lived, so we interrupt
The journey, Ali Farka Toure, something
Of griot, something of blues singer,
An ikon, an ambassador, an export
Harmony in a time of tribal discord.

We drag through Niafunke's sand filled streets.
The heat would melt a candle or a tyre.
There's nothing in the kiosks here to buy
Though we'd love some Toure dvds.
The waiter in a bar tells us that his
Son is playing with the band tonight for true
And offers counterfeit CDs he claims are new.

'What about you Ruth? You haven't talked
About your life.' Jay wipes his mouth of fat
The chips were fried in, pointing with his fork,
'I'd like to know just where you're at.
Where you started out, this and that.'
Her fingers rake the beaded dreads apart
'OK, the beers are on their way, I'll start.

'You think fairy stories stay in books,
With magic, wizards, good and evil witches.
Strange fates can't happen now; good luck
As grace granted through blest wishes
Blown by angels. This has us in stitches,
Laughing at babushka superstitions
The wiles of charlatans and trick magicians.

'Well, Lawrence was a scholar in the work of Pope
Deconstructing reference and strophe.
He lived still with his mother, had no wife,
The modern world had hardly touched his life.
He gently mocked the undergrad pretensions
Of his students, but gave them full attention.
One icy day he heard a high-pitched cry.
He looked around the quilted, snow cloud sky
But the wailing and distress increased.
Had the call box trapped a wretched beast?
He looked and saw a lump of dingy cloth
And tiny hands a flutter like two moths.
The screaming made him press his hands to ears
Not used to baby's piercing screams and tears.
Frost patterned all the windows, lacy glass.
The new born thing would die if he walked past.
He lifted up the sodden infant, held
It deep inside his coat; his heart unravelled.
As he walked the screaming came to end.
The baby sucked his woolly jumpers' threads.
Unbuttoning his coat when he got home
His mum thought he'd brought back a tome
Of poetry but saw a hungry, baby girl
Her wobbling head, a nest of wiry curls
And milky dark blue eyes and coffee skin.
She held it in her gnarled, arthritic fin
And cooed and rocked. She'd known
She'd never have a grandchild from her son.
The ambulance was called and thus my life
Was saved. Because he didn't have a wife
Adoption was not possible but Ruth's
the name he gave me, you've deduced.
I was given to a couple of mixed race.
My dad was African, mum white, they'd space
For one more child, a sister to their daughter
Five years old. She couldn't have another
And for children she had love to spare.
Lawrence came to call upon his bairn
His aisling and held me in his scholar's arms
And wondered as I grew from tot to girl
How personality is gradually unfurled.

He'd take me out to concerts, shows and plays
And bought me books as presents on birthdays
Like a kindly granddad from another age
Or a wise man from the East, a sage.
But things were falling fast apart at home.
My father liked to visit back. He slalomed
Down between his roots and life in Chester.
We didn't know he'd fathered children there
In Ghana. This secret pulled apart
Our lives, collapsing like a house of cards.
My older sister brought no consolation.
Her jealousy of me was not on ration.
I was a cuckoo in the terraced nest
Who'd used up too much parents' love, a guest
Who'd overstayed her welcome. By stealth
She'd work to keep her mother to herself.
Our mum was tired of how we fought.
I drifted off to Amsterdam and sought
Distraction in messing up my mind
Also started searching in the records
For the girl who might have given birth
But a foundling leaves no notes, no stats.
Though I placed adverts, I got nothing back.

'But through this Lawrence made me look
Ahead and see that when you stayed stuck
In the past you lost the joy of finding new
Directions – so chucked self-pity and threw
The dice. It's kids a lot worse off than me I'm
Perking up – youth who've drifted into crime.

Part IX

The *pinasse* docks. We're here. A 4x4 to ride
To a hotel with toilets, showers too
And there at six foot six our Tuareg guide
With dagger in his belt, his turban blue
With indigo, his flowing, spotless bubu.
There's a scramble for the seats by him
Elbow in elbow, force of limb on limb.

The sand filled roads are lined with offices
Of NGOs and charities – the houses mud-built
And the mosques; the city incandesces
In the dusk, turning red and ochre, gilded
Sunset but no gold lined pavements – just silted
Up with sand, the legendary city
Which the desert grips, no drop of pity.

Timbuktu – once fabled source of gold
Sought by mercenaries, soldiers of chance
But here they found its legend oversold
Nothing but the mud built streets and sand.
We check in to the hotel and demand
Our rooms, flush toilets and hot showers,
Switch on our lights and waste electric power.

The evening has us looking for a bar.
We leave Tony to his silent phone.
The local kids have T-shirts – regular,
Small and large with the legend sewn
Across – *Been to Timbuktu*. We moan
About the price – the kids can truly fleece
Us in the multi languages they speak.

Tuareg salesmen ply us with their wares–
Silver trinkets, blankets, leather bags.
Renee brings our guide along – her Coeur
Is taken and she buys him stuff. He'll brag
To others what she spent, sell the silver swag
For cash – that is what he needs – and tries
To blarney her with low-pitched, luscious lies.

Everything we eat is scarred with grit.
We visit the antiquities and photo mosques
and decorated wooden doors like other tourists
From Moscow, Beijing and Bangkok
Or Tokyo – descending like a flock
Looking for bewitchment and appeal
But find its people short of their next meal.

'You might like to take a camel ride
With me,' says Dieter speaking to the timid
Tony worried the police won't try to find
His wife or whether bandit gangsters kid-
napped Chris and will eventually get rid
Of her when they find out he's got no hoard
Of money for a ransom or reward.

Dieter wants to buy some antique goods
From Tuareg villages beyond the town.
Camels decked in saddles made of wood
Are seated on the sand – their guide in gown
And turban leads them gently northbound
And Tony spots a harrier-hawk in flight,
His troubles swallowed up in his delight.

Fateha goes off to buy a hand-carved chest
Of sandalwood – she has an eye for beauty
And looks for elegance and skill, the best
There is – Finn will carry back her booty
Out of chivalry and not a sense of duty.
She'll find a way to get it on the plane
And then to her Victorian house in Staines.

Rick as he walks around the streets snarling
At the hawkers who would sell him knick knacks
Puzzles how Inez could be his darling.
Could he downsize? Cover up his precious tracks?
Buy her antique Songhai bric a brac?
How can he make this woman with such spirit
See he's fun and not a loud-mouthed bigot?

'I wonder where our Martin's been,' says Ruth
'He hasn't come on any trips – no sign at all.'
'I share his room,' says Lee 'to tell the truth
He isn't back till late – drives me up the wall.
He says he wants to travel on to Senegal.'
'Perhaps he's found a lover,' Our Ruth guesses
'I hope he's being rational not reckless.'

'Did I see you dancing in the club?' she says
'With a woman dressed in sumptuous
Robes?' Lee nods his head. 'Don't tell Inez.
She's so canny. Hambo introduced us.
She seems dead keen. I think she really likes us.'
'Be careful Lee she might be after life
In England.' 'Who cares? Time I had a wife.'

And so the days of sojourn must now cease
The travellers return to former roles.
Exotic scenes will fade to memories
Captured in the frozen moments told
At parties, but coloured in and oversold.
For now Inez confirms the flight and bookings
To Bamako on the ancient Ilyushin.

The tourists gather up their fancy presents
And squash them into leather bags with wheels.
Renee hasn't seen Koguem since she spent
Her money in the markets. But what she feels
Is stripped off with the face-pack that she peels.
Dieter calculates the profit to be won
In Rheinaue flea-market fair in Bonn.

The ancient plane takes off and looking down
The tourists see the Delta's veins fan out
Emerald green against the desert's burnt brown
Canvas – shrinking as the climate roasts.
The source of life unless in time of drought.
We film and photograph through grimy glass
A haunting, fragile beauty – then it's past.

Ruth rests her head upon the shoulder
Of guess who? Yes, he's won her cautious trust.
She likes his crinkled face even though it's older
Than hers, well-lived and mischievous.
Mute Tony thinks of gangs who're dangerous
Wonders if she's hostage to either
Disgruntled Tuaregs or Al Queida?

Thoughts about the missing, unmissed Chris
Also cross the mind of lawyer Rick
But briefly as he's frying other fish.
Taking Inez out to dinner at a hand-picked
Restaurant requires a switch in politics.
Mike muses on the Jasmine situation.
Perhaps she's just a flavourful flirtation.

Fateha knows that Finn's soft eyes
Are watching her as she gazes through
The windows on savannah as it rises
To the mountains in the south and the blue
Green river curving like a snake tattoo.
There are so many differences she thinks.
Would her parents like a son-in-law who drinks?

When she lands she'll take the local train
That growls through tunnels black with soot
Climb up steps into the grey street, rain
Filled clouds, pale faces, the light like stewed
Tea. She'll get her keys out – they lie mute
Upon her palm. This world seems spent,
Like the end of Ramadan or Lent.

She'll step inside her stripped-pine, white-washed hall
Clogged with post and ads for take-aways.
She'll see the rows of masks upon the walls
The antique carvings from exotic places
Half remembered – she'll feel appalled
By all those devil masks and sullen grins
And see at once the tender face of Finn.

She'll wait a day or two but then she'll call
His number and his voice will reassure
That the gentleness of the very tall
Is there on offer – a man who'll cure
Her loneliness, a love that will endure.
Unlike our Tony who has stayed
Waiting for a ransom he can't pay.